This Is My Body

This Is My Body
A Guide to the Mass

Ian Petit, O.S.B.

Illustrated by
Elizabeth Ruth Obbard

A Liturgical Press Book

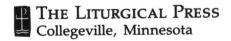

THE LITURGICAL PRESS
Collegeville, Minnesota

Cover design by David Manahan, O.S.B.
Woodcut detail, c. 1480; National Gallery of Art, Cologne

First published in 1991 by Darton, Longman and Todd Ltd., London.

This edition published in 1993 by The Liturgical Press, Collegeville, Minnesota. Printed in the United States of America.

1	2	3	4	5	6	7	8	9

Library of Congress Cataloging-in-Publication Data
Petit, Ian.
   This is my body / Ian Petit ; illustrated by Elizabeth Ruth
Obbard.
      p.   cm.
   Originally published: London : Darton, Longman, and Todd,
c1991.
   ISBN 0-8146-2133-3
   1. Lord's Supper—Catholic Church. 2. Mass. 3. Catholic Church-
-Doctrines. 4. Catholic Church—Liturgy.   I. Title.
BX2230.2.P47   1993
264'.02036—dc20   92-43983
                                                             CIP

Contents

Acknowledgements

The Scripture quotations in this publication are based on *The Jerusalem Bible* published and copyright 1966, 1967 and 1968 by Darton, Longman and Todd Ltd and Doubleday and Co. Inc. Excerpts from the English translation of *The Roman Missal* are copyright 1973, International Committee on English in the Liturgy, Inc. All rights reserved.

Preface

The burst of glory that takes place, when the body and blood of the Lord are made present on the altar, cannot be known by the senses, nor can it be grasped by the mind. What has happened is so beyond the human realm of experience or understanding, that it can only be accepted on the authority of God. It is by faith that we accept our Lord's stark words, 'This is my body – this is my blood'. Once we start trying to understand how this can be, we get lost in endless human speculation. It is true, it can be argued that perhaps the Lord did not mean us to take his words literally, as when he talked about cutting off our right hand when it scandalizes us; but there are enough texts about eating and drinking his body and blood to suggest that he meant what he said.

Faith is beyond reason, not opposed to it. Our senses and our minds remain untouched; but faith tells us that we stand before the most important event in the history of the world. We stand present before the mystery of Christ; we are made present to the One who died for our sins and rose to new life so that we might live in a new way. All the hosts of heaven are prostrate around us, worshipping before this mystery where the One who is died for those who once were not. In the midst of this company we stand blind in our senses, uncomprehending in our minds. If we could but grasp the holiness of the moment made present to us, we, too, would lie face down calling out, 'Holy, holy is the Lord God of hosts'.

The Mass, though, has become very familiar to us, and I am reminded of a conversation I once had with a Hindu who was playing the part of Christ in a Mystery play. He came to attend Mass, and afterwards he remarked, 'But, how can you say it so quickly?' Actually that Mass had been rather reflective and slow, but I learnt much from his observation. He had found a profound sense of awe in playing the role of Christ in a play, and I began to reflect that if we really believe what is happening at Mass, why have many of us allowed it to become so familiar?

I fear we were introduced to the sign before comprehending the awesomeness of the reality behind that sign. This has certainly been true of me. From an early age, I believed the Mass to be important. I learnt how to follow it in my missal, and felt a certain pleasure in being able to be on the right page at the right time – but this did not bring the Mass alive for me.

It was only late in my life that I began to understand that 'to live' the gospel did not mean 'to practise the gospel precepts', but it meant to accept what Christ had done for me through his death and resurrection and be transformed by that truth. This gave me new life, this enabled me to live in a new way. Once I began to grasp the truth, I began to see that the Mass was the 're-presenting' of the saving event to us so that its mighty power may continue to affect us.

Much could be written on the Mass, and I have neither desire nor capability to write an exhaustive treatise or a history on it. I have wanted to share some insights and thoughts that I have had over the years in the hope that the Holy Spirit will breathe light into truths both old and new. I pray that as you read these pages and as you ponder the meaning of the Mass you will sense something of that burst of glory that envelops the whole of the worshipping family, drawing us all into the very holiness of God himself.

1

The Reality Behind the Sign

The spirit world cannot be felt, sensed or pictured. In it there is no space, no size, no colour. It is beyond our mind, beyond our grasp, beyond our senses.

A spiritual person is one who acknowledges that such a world exists. There are no convincing arguments for or against it; it is as though a decision is made, for some good reason, to believe or not to believe.

There is a knowing that does not come from proof, a certainty that does not result from arguments. Today, after a period when the spiritual world has been denied, there is a rediscovery of the spiritual dimension. This book deals with spiritual truth.

My Experience of the Mass

From my earliest days, I was told that the Mass was important, and because I trusted my parents and elders, I accepted what they said as true. I did not find very much satisfaction in it personally, but I had been told it was important, so it was important to me. I knew, in some way, it represented Calvary, but I found it hard to connect what I saw happening on the altar with what I knew happened outside the walls of Jerusalem. I also believed that Jesus came to me at the time of communion, and that, of course, meant a great deal.

My schooling days coincided with a time when it was thought good and proper for students to attend daily Mass. I cannot recall ever resenting that, even though I did not seem to draw much from it. It was something good Catholics did and I really did not give it all that much thought.

Such daily attendance of Mass by schoolchildren may seem surprising, but we need to remember that the scene then was very different from what it is today. Then, the Roman Catholic Church sought to keep a society of its own, subsisting in another society which was either Christian or non-Christian. Today, things have changed. In the western world there are many who are no longer Christian, and the Catholic Church, instead of trying to keep a closed society, is opening dialogue with modern-day thought. This has dismantled many of the bulwarks that protected the faithful, and it calls for the ordinary Catholic to be much more discerning and responsible.

The general upheaval has caused many new and

interesting ideas to be accessible to ordinary Catholics; and while this is good for it brings us out of the ghetto mentality by which we can be so protected that we jog along living on secondhand truths, it can also be harmful if we do not have a good, solid understanding of the basic Christian message as a foundation to our lives.

All this has produced considerable confusion and I see a need for solid teaching, especially with regard to fundamental gospel truths. As a priest, I meet today many who are literally lost because of all that has happened in the Church over these last thirty years. I think they are lost because the foundation truths were never securely laid. All too often we presume that these truths have been firmly grasped, when in fact that is far from the case.

We can be quite secure in belonging to a closed society, but when that society ceases to be closed, we can have a sense of being rudderless. All sorts of options now seem available, and while that can be good for the wise and discerning, it can be very unhelpful for the lost and confused. Frequently, it seems to me, the Mass is a cause for worry. Once it was in Latin, and that made it mysterious, but now that it is in the vernacular, people complain that the mystery has disappeared. But the mystery of the Mass is not in the language, it is in the making present of the sacrifice of Jesus on Calvary. I find that many people have not been well trained in the Scriptures which tell about the saving work of Jesus. If the saving work of Jesus has not been firmly grasped, then the re-presenting of that work under signs, will only be seen as signs and they will lack their full content.

What Do We Mean by Sacraments?

Sacraments are not magic. They are God's way of making his Son's redeeming work available to everyone. I sometimes wonder if many of us were introduced to the sacraments, the signs, and somehow never reached the reality behind those signs. We can be over-sacramentalized, and by that I mean that the importance of the sign can overshadow the reality. We all learnt the significance of Baptism, Confession, Mass and Holy Communion – but did we understand how the saving work of Christ was being administered to us through these different sacraments? Were we approaching the sacrament or the reality? I am well aware of the problem of communicating these truths to children, but I know from my own experience I never really understood the sacramental system until far too late in life.

In the gospel story of the woman with the haemorrhage who approached Jesus from behind, intending to touch the hem of his garment and be healed without drawing notice to herself, we are taught that although many were touching the Lord, it was the woman who had faith who was healed. So it is with sacraments, they are not magic – we have to approach with faith in what Jesus has done. We may receive the sacrament legitimately, but we can limit its effect by our lack of faith.

On the other hand it needs to be pointed out that although the woman had faith she was not healed until she had touched the Lord. Sacraments are the moment when we touch the Lord so that his saving work, which has been already achieved, floods into us. This makes it very important for us to know and understand the Lord's work of salvation and then rejoice that we can receive it into ourselves through the signs he has left us.

Salvation is not something that we achieve ourselves, it is something we allow God to achieve in us. God's way of achieving it is through the death and resurrection of his Son. By dying and rising, Christ has broken the power of sin over our lives and enabled us to live in a new way. We can now live 'in Christ', rather than in our own strength. This is God's way of salvation and when we accept his way, which is not easy for it means renouncing all self-glory, then, through faith and the sacraments, the great work of Christ can begin to affect us. We need a firm understanding of this central truth if we are going to appreciate the gift of the Mass.

Two Saving Events

There are two great saving events in Scripture, one belongs to the Old Testament – when Moses led the Hebrews out of Egypt; the other belongs to the New Testament – when Jesus died on Calvary.

In the Old Testament story, after God had delivered the Hebrews from bondage in Egypt, they were told never to forget what the Lord had done for them.

> The Lord has brought you into the land which he swore to your fathers Abraham, Isaac and Jacob that he would give you. . . Then take care you do not forget the Lord your God who brought you out of the land of Egypt, out of the house of

13

slavery . . . In times to come, when your son asks
you, 'What is the meaning of the decrees and
laws and customs that the Lord God has laid
down for you?' you shall tell your son, 'Once we
were Pharaoh's slaves in Egypt, and the Lord
God brought us out of Egypt by his mighty hand.
Before our eyes the Lord God worked great and
terrible signs and wonders against Egypt, against
Pharaoh and all his House. And he brought us
out from there to lead us into the land he swore
to our fathers he would give to us.'

Deut 6:10, 12, 20–23

Not only were they to remember, constantly call to
mind and teach this great deliverance that God had
wrought for them, they were, each year, to re-enact
what had happened. They were not to go through
the same deliverance, but they were to call it to
mind by ritual. They were to gather in families,
dress as though they were going on a journey, slay
an unblemished lamb and eat a meal similar to the
one they were ordered to eat before the Exodus
began. In this way they would bring the event so
vividly to mind, that it would affect them afresh.
This would keep their gratitude ever present and
alive, and so they would not forget the goodness of
God.

It was God who initiated the journey. The Hebrews did not decide to embark upon it. It was not
planned, it was not a journey for gaining self-
reliance, self-improvement – it was a journey
decided upon by God, whereby he would transform
his stiff-necked people. He would make them into
a people who would trust him no matter what. In

the desert all support was taken from them; they were faced with either perishing or trusting in God! God was forming his people in a rough school, so that when they entered the Promised Land, they would still trust in him and not in their new found wealth. Hence, in the Promised Land, there was an absolute need to remind themselves of what God had done for them, and to remind themselves forcibly, so that they might trust God rather than their arms, wealth or abundance.

In the New Testament Jesus said, 'Do this in memory of me' (Luke 22:19). He had just turned wine into his blood and bread into his body, demonstrating what was to happen on Calvary – his body and blood would be separated causing death. In the Mass, we make both Jesus' body and blood present, and thus we make his saving event present to us. We do not repeat it, we make ourselves present to this eternal happening. In other words, we call to mind the New Testament's saving event, just as the Hebrews called to mind their saving event – the Exodus from Egypt. We do this for many reasons; one is that we will never forget it, another is that its saving power will still be applied to us.

Of all the events of the New Testament, the most central and important is that Jesus took our sins upon himself on Calvary and paid the penalty by dying. The death that he entered was unable to hold this innocent One, so the Father called his beloved, obedient Son back out of death. Jesus did not come back to life in the same way that Lazarus did; Lazarus was resuscitated, Jesus rose to new life. He did not return to what he had been before. He was new, yet different, the same Jesus but alive in a new way. Here was the One from whom the new race of humans would spring, and anyone who now believes in him can share in this new life. This is the great truth that we call to mind at every Mass and celebrate with prayers of wonder and thanksgiving. I will return to this truth many times in the course of this book.

From the earliest of times the Church has gathered together to fulfil the Lord's command – 'Do this in memory of me'. Our earliest record of this comes from Justin the Martyr. He wrote around AD 150, and described how people would come from different areas to gather in one place. There they would listen to readings either from the apostles or one of the prophets. This was followed by a short address given by the one presiding. Prayers were said, then bread and wine were brought and presented; the president gave thanks and all said 'Amen'. Then the eucharistic gifts were distributed, and the deacons were sent to bring them to those who could not be present.

Today we follow the same pattern – there are prayers and readings, bread and wine are offered, we give thanks to God and do what the Lord told us to do – we break bread and say the very words he said and make his body present to us; we do the same with the wine making his blood present, thus symbolizing his death whereby his body and blood were separated. The death and rising of Christ is the very means by which God has rescued us, and we celebrate its truth and ponder its deep meaning as it becomes present to us. We will never ponder its full significance, and so time and again we come before this mystery and allow ourselves to be caught up in its power and healing. Over the centuries the prayers and readings have become set, not in a static sense, but rather because over the years, in well chosen words, they have distilled the deep meaning of God's love for us.

Having made ourselves present to the saving work of Christ, we then do what Christ commanded us to do – we eat his body and drink his blood. 'For my flesh is real food and my blood is real drink. He who eats my flesh and drinks my blood lives in me and I live in him' (Jn 6:56). A Christian is someone who lives in Christ and allows Christ to live in him. There is a difference between 'having' life and 'living' life. It is one thing to have Christ 'in' us, another to allow him 'to live in' us.

The saving work of Christ has been completed. Jesus' last words were, 'It is finished' (Jn 19:30). Yet this work has not been completed as far as we are concerned, and not yet begun for those still to be born. This is the task of the Holy Spirit – to reveal who Christ is and what he has done for us by his death and resurrection; and as we accept these truths in an ever deeper way, the Spirit causes the work of Jesus to affect us more radically. In the Eucharist we have the very central work of Christ, his death and resurrection, made present to us, and we are given the extraordinary privilege of being exposed to this saving event, offering it in thanksgiving to the Father and then receiving as food and drink the very body and blood of the Lord so that his life in us may be strong and active.

Again this is not to make us holy in the sense that we accumulate holy virtues, holy ways of doing things, as though we become holy in ourselves. God alone is holy, and we are holy only in so far as we are in him. God's plan is not that we set out on 'virtue gathering courses', but that we allow him to transform us into the image of his Son. As the Hebrews were called to make a journey that they did not plan or even want, so, too, we will be led, as Peter, where we would rather not go. God has a plan for our life, our work is to allow him his way. 'Come follow me' – the way he went was a way of self-giving, a pouring out, a losing, a wasting. 'Do this in memory of me.'

2

You Gather a People to Yourself

There is so much more to being a Christian than our personal salvation. When we become Christians we enter a family, we join a body, we become members of the Church. This is not the same as being a member of a club; we are actually grafted onto the body of Christ, and become living members, sharing in his life with all the other members. Just as any part of the human body needs to remain in the body if it is to stay alive, so, too, a Christian is committed to unity with the other members.

We do not go to Mass because we feel like going. We go because we are called. God calls us to come together as the body of his Son and offer to the Father the most perfect offering that could be made, the very offering of Christ himself. We do not choose the members of our natural family, so neither do we choose the members of the Church. In a parish we are given our brothers and sisters in

21

Christ. All the faithful have a right to be there and we are all equal before the Lord. Earthly differences are of no consequence.

Now that the Mass is in the vernacular, and there are 'folk' and 'traditional' Masses, there can be a tendency to go shopping for one that suits our taste. While this is understandable, it does cut at the sense of parish being the local body of Christ. The Mass is the Mass no matter what form it takes. There may be a need for a parish to consider carefully whether its form of Mass is the most helpful, but it is sad when a parish divides and people end up by going to this church or that and have no commitment to the other members who worship with them. We are called to be a people who are alive with the life of the Risen Lord; we do not just happen to use the same building; we are not like people who use the same restaurant.

Introduction to the Mass

The Mass begins with a simple preparation. The first thing we do is to make the sign of the Cross. By this gesture we remind ourselves of the three Persons of the Trinity, calling to mind the Father who so loved the world that he sent his Son; the Son who out of love for the Father and the world came to bear the sins of the world, and thus save the world; and the Holy Spirit who continuously is coming to us to make effective in us the plan of the Father made possible by the Son's obedience.

The priest then greets the people who have gathered together from many different parts, thus forming the body of Christ, so that they can offer the

Father worthy praise and worship. Many talents and gifts will be required to make this gathering fruitful. There will be readers, who are to proclaim the Word of God. Reading at Mass involves much more than reading the Word of God aloud. The Word of God is something alive, and if we just read it as a piece of reading, then we may well prevent the message from reaching the people gathered there. I believe it is important for the congregation to pray that the reader be anointed by the Spirit of God, so that hearts may be moved. The readers, in their turn, need to appreciate the solemn privilege of being the mouthpiece for God's Word.

There will also be those who enrich the service with their singing, and again how important it is to see that this is not a performance; in some way the singing must bring people actually to worship God. Then there will be those who serve, those who take collections, those who welcome people, those who assist with the children of the parish. There are many duties to perform to help this body come before the Lord. The priest's solemn role is to bring the Holy Spirit down on our own gifts, transforming them into the sacrifice of Christ, and together with the people to offer that to the Father.

All these different roles show that we form together the body of Christ, we are not individuals on individual journeys, we belong to each other, we share a new life together. Because we fail to live this extraordinary truth, we are invited at the beginning of the Mass to confess our sins to God and one another.

I was once present at a Mass in Rome where a Central American bishop was the main celebrant.

He reminded us of how easy it is to give responses by rote without much thought for the meaning behind them. For example, it is so easy to reply to the invitation, 'Lift up your hearts', with, 'We've lifted them up to the Lord', and yet have our hearts anything but lifted up. He then suggested that we had an opportunity now to mean what we were going to say. He told us that we were about to say, 'I confess to Almighty God, and to you, my brothers and sisters, that I have sinned'. 'Would you please turn to the brother or sister on your left and right, and confess a sin,' were his next words. You can imagine the panic that broke out. If I had known that this was going to happen, I would have made sure where I stood and who would be next to me. The result actually was very moving. Having dared to say something to our neighbour, and it did not have to be anything very startling, we all sensed our common need for God's forgiveness. This united us and we went into that eucharistic celebration sensing very much our oneness, and when we asked for God's mercy our prayer was heartfelt.

On feast days the 'Gloria' is said or sung – a beautiful prayer which celebrates the sheer goodness of God. We thank him for being who he is. We bless him, we honour him, we worship him. Here is prayer which is all God-ward. Petition is present, but we do not focus on it, rather our sense of God's great glory makes us aware of our shallowness and so we call out to him to 'hear our prayer'. In our own private prayers it can be helpful to create our own 'gloria' and to think of all the reasons we have for praising God.

Following the reconciliation, and the 'Gloria' if

there is one, the priest leads us in a prayer, a prayer that is shaped by and takes into account the liturgical season that we are in. For example, during Advent we focus on the Lord's coming, so the prayer during that season talks of the different 'comings' of Jesus. He has come in history, he needs to come continually to us in a personal way, and there is his final coming in glory. We use this season to remind ourselves how much the Chosen People longed for his coming, and to stir ourselves also to long with ardour for the Lord.

During Lent the flavour of the prayer is repentance and sorrow for sin, and as we approach Holy Week we reflect on the mystery of the suffering and death of Christ. All this helps us to appreciate the Father's wondrous plan for our salvation.

I was once saying Mass in the USA, and when I said to the people, 'Let us pray,' to my astonishment they all burst into vocal prayer. Then I realized that I had invited them to pray. This helped me to understand why the prayer said at that time in the Mass is called the 'collect' – the priest's prayer collects the prayers of the people together.

This introductory part to the Mass is a simple preparation for entering into the Mass proper, where we start by listening to God's Word.

3

Speak, Lord, Your Servant is Listening

The basic format for the Mass has remained virtually unchanged over the centuries. There are readings taken from the Word of God, readings which link the Mass to the synagogue gatherings, and then comes the breaking of bread, introducing the Lord's gift to his Church.

In the early days the readings were not arranged as they are today. Then the reader simply read as long as there was time or it seemed appropriate. Today, on Sundays or feast days, there are three readings and these are chosen to fit in with the liturgical season. The first reading is normally taken from the Old Testament, but this is replaced by one from the Acts of the Apostles during Paschal time. The second reading comes from one of the letters of the New Testament. The third reading is a gospel passage. During Advent, Christmas, Lent and Paschal time all three readings are linked; but in ordinary time this is only true of the first reading and the gospel. The second reading then works through one of the epistles giving appropriate sections each Sunday.

Jews gathered in the synagogue primarily to hear God's law proclaimed, and to learn about this God who had adopted the Jews as his chosen people and had worked such marvels for their deliverance.

The Jewish people had a great reverence for the Word of God. The Word of God, spoken and then written down on stone tablets or scrolls, was God's presence among them. The early Christians wanted to keep this reading aloud of Scripture because it was important for knowing God and learning the plan he had for his people; and, besides, it helped keep a link between the Jewish custom and the development of Christianity. It was also a very fitting preparation for the breaking of bread.

In some Protestant churches you will not see the altar in the centre but rather a pulpit with the book of Scriptures enshrined upon it. In many Catholic churches the tabernacle is in the centre with the altar, though since Vatican II there has been a return to the practice whereby the Blessed Sacrament is reserved in a side chapel, leaving the altar of sacrifice in the middle. Also since Vatican II the book of Scriptures is enthroned in the sanctuary. At solemn Masses it is carried in at the beginning, held high, and, before the reading, carried in procession with reverence and dignity. The changes since Vatican II are not radical innovations, rather they are a return to how things once were. God comes to us and is present in both Word and Sacrament.

The Word liturgy is an important part of the Mass for through it we allow God to speak to us so that we might respond to him. We Catholics have not been well grounded in our Scriptures, and we need to take advantage of the books and courses now available to help us understand God's Word. We are not all asked to be scholars, but we are called to listen to God's Word and be formed by it as we obey it.

Old Testament

The books of the Old Testament can be quite a stumbling block because God can appear a bit temperamental, at times very angry and causing terrible catastrophes, then repenting and promising all sorts of blessings to his people. It is important, though, to remember that the authors are describing God as they perceived him, and not as he really is. No idea that we have of God, is God. Our ideas of him are very limited and over the years they change. All of us have thought of God in different ways, at some times we have imagined him benign, at others, cruel, distant, near, loving or frightening. Life is a pilgrimage – a getting to know God. Older people may smile when they remember some of the ways they used to think about God. Time and experience have caused them to change their ideas.

This is why it is important to listen to the Word of God over and over again, for as we change, so we hear the Word differently. The Word, by itself, will not always change us because we can develop a set frame of mind whereby we prevent the Word entering in to transform us. This is where we need the touch of the Lord through the sacraments, setting us free to hear his Word. In the Mass we celebrate both the Word touching us through Scripture and touching us through sacrament.

The Chosen People had to grow in their understanding of God. To start off with they had simple and uncomplicated ideas. They understood that God was good and wanted them to be good also, and naturally they concluded that if they were good then God would bless them. God had to lead them beyond this tit for tat relationship; he had to reveal to them that there was more to life than prosperous farms and large families. They were in danger of viewing their relationship with him in very selfish terms. All this could develop into a selfish friendship. Slowly they began to see that good people could also suffer and evil people prosper. As they wrestled with these difficulties, men were inspired to write about them.

The book of Job, for example, attempts to explain why the good suffer. Satan had complained to God that no wonder Job was such a God-fearing person, he had every blessing he could have wished for. Satan asked permission to strike at his possessions, and when that did not make Job curse God, he attacked his person. The story is fiction, but it has truths to teach. Job's friends all come and argue that he must have sinned against God. Job contends that he is innocent, but towards the end of the book he complains that God has been a bit hard on him. Job is ticked off by God for questioning him, and the story ends with Job being reinstated with even more blessings and wealth. It does not answer the problem of suffering, but it wrestles with it.

Sections from different books of the Old Testament are drawn upon according to the liturgical season. Isaiah features a great deal during Advent with his more apocalyptical passages being used to direct our gaze towards the Lord who has come and who is still to come. During Lent readings are taken from a variety of books illustrating the unfaithfulness of God's people and their need for repentance. All this is to direct our thoughts to our own relationship with God.

Psalms

After the first reading there is the responsorial psalm. Here the Church asks us to respond to the first reading by putting a psalm on our lips. You will notice that this psalm is connected to the reading we have just heard. It is not just any old psalm chosen at random. It responds to the message of the first reading. In doing this the Church is teaching us to respond, not just with our lips, but also with our hearts. This is why we need to listen to what we are saying or singing, and not give responses parrot-fashion.

New Testament

The epistles and the gospels tell us what God has done for us through the life, death and resurrection of Jesus – that through Christ's death and resurrection, sin has been forgiven and a new life has begun, a life which we draw from Christ. We need to keep this thought in our minds while we listen to these readings.

Not every reading we listen to will talk specifically of the death and resurrection of Christ. With regard to the gospels, more often than not we listen to accounts of the miracles of Christ or some teaching that he gave. But unless our minds have the central message of the gospel clearly fixed in them, we will listen to the readings and miss the point of what we are hearing. We may well admire the story, be moved with wonder at his power and concern, but never connect that this same Jesus is alive today, and therefore can minister to us as well. He who gave new sight to the blind, can give us, who are so spiritually blind, new sight to see the truth. Too often we imagine these gifts are for the 'holy', the 'good'.

So, when we read the gospels we are not just looking back to the time of Christ and seeing what he did at that time as though we were reading a bit of history. Nor are we being told, 'This is how to live, now you get on with it'. Rather we are reminding ourselves that this same Jesus is alive and working amongst us today, and that he wants us to live in his strength, not our own. If, for example, the day's reading focuses on Jesus' teaching about love of our neighbour, we could listen to it, and then go off and try to put it into practice, and get thoroughly frustrated by our inability to love. This could lead to discouragement or feelings of guilt and failure. It would hardly be good news, and we might be tempted to give up on Christianity if it seemed to bring nothing but struggle and frustration. But the gospel message is not meant to send us off trying to fulfil its teachings in our own power, it is seeking to show us who Jesus is and that it is only in him that we can be fruitful. This is why we must listen to the gospel reading, knowing in our hearts the basic message.

The epistles, especially St Paul's, are more complex. Often the authors are writing about situations which we, unless we are historians, do not understand. They are dealing with problems that have arisen in the early Christian communities, and reading these letters without too much background can be confusing. As the apostles spread the news of Jesus, they kept in touch with the cities where they had made converts. The letters they wrote are known as the epistles. In these letters we see the 'Church' trying to explain the teachings about Jesus Christ. They are a fund of deep insights into the mystery of Christ. A number are written by men who knew the Lord both before and after his resurrection and were present when the Holy Spirit came down with such power and might. Again the good news of Jesus Christ is being spelled out to us showing how it is a development, and not a contradiction, of the Jewish teachings. Again the message is that through Christ's death and resurrection, sin has been forgiven and a new life has been given to enable us to live in a new way.

Paul claimed to have learnt his understanding of Christ through a revelation and not from the other apostles. The great theme, which he deals with, is that observance of the law does not save us. We are saved by belief in Jesus Christ. The Jews had been brought up to live a life dependent on God. This life of dependence on God was illustrated by the kind of life that the law laid down. The law said, 'A man of God will live like this'. It is easy to see how this changed into, 'If I live that sort of life, then I must be a man of God'.

Fallen man is unable to live such a life, so the law of God became, not a means of being set free, but a proof that mankind is not free. It showed man's need of healing. God, in the prophet Ezekiel, promised man a new heart and God's own spirit. Jesus is the new man with the new heart and God's own spirit. The New Testament calls us to believe in Jesus Christ and receive a new heart and spirit from him.

These basic truths are of utmost importance because they help us listen to the Word of God with some understanding of God's plans for the human race. Because for much of my life my ideas of God had been very faulty, I found the Word confusing, obscure and irrelevant. It just did not touch me, or it made me feel fearful and very inadequate. After some considerable time I slowly came to realize that God is on my side, that he loves me and has sent his Son that I might live a new life in him. Only as I began to grasp the real message of the gospel did I find the Word helpful and full of meaning.

Our Response to the Word

We will all hear the Word of God as individuals. God speaks to each of us where we are. That is why it can be so fruitful when we share what each of us has heard. The Word of God can correct us, encourage us, enlighten us. It is not meant to fill us with despair.

Having listened to the Word, we are now ready to enter into the action of the Mass. The readings will have shown us our need of God; either we will want to thank him and dedicate our lives to him, or we will want to say sorry and ask him to change us, or we will just want to place ourselves in his safe-keeping. All this fits us for the next main stage in the Mass where we will offer ourselves to God under the signs of bread and wine.

Homily

On Sundays, after the gospel, the priest gives a homily. A homily is not a sermon, a homily gives light to the readings. It is meant to help the people grasp the message of what has been read. It is important that the congregation pray for the priest and ask that he will truly break the Word of God for them, that he will put the readings in context and show what is being said to them today. At the end of the homily every one stands to declare their faith in the triune God.

4

We Believe

We can easily imagine that saying something by rote is the same as saying it by heart. But to say something by rote means saying the words without thought to their meaning, whereas to say something by heart means assenting with our hearts to what we say with our lips.

When we say the Creed, or any prayer for that matter, it is important that we listen to what we say, so as to allow our hearts to assent. In the Creed we list our beliefs in God and his actions.

'We believe in one God.' As a body we state our belief. We are not a lot of individuals proclaiming our personal faith; we state that we, as one body, believe in one God. None of us causes our own existence, it is God who calls us into being, therefore we all share a common origin. God is the One who is, we are the ones who once were not. We share this common ground with all creation. Our value is not because of what we do, our value is because the One who makes us does not make mistakes.

God is not just our creator, he is our Father because of our union with Christ Jesus, and we affirm him as Father and Almighty. He is not our Father by nature, but by adoption; that is, he has chosen us to be his children and given us new life as children of God.

We also affirm our belief in the Son of God, who springs eternally from the Father. The Son is not the Father, yet he is co-equal to the Father. This is a deep mystery, which our minds, confined to think within the limits of time and space, cannot grasp. We also state our belief that the Son was involved in the creation of all things. The Father spoke his Word and things happened. The Word of God is his Son, hence 'through him all things were made'.

All these affirmations refer to the mysterious relationship between the Father and the Son. We then confess our belief in God's plan for us creatures wounded by sin. We acknowledge that God so loved the world that he sent his only Son into this world to save it. We accept the extraordinary truth that through the power of the Holy Spirit God's Son took flesh in the womb of a virgin and became one of the human family. Jesus did this so that he might repair the damage incurred by the human race when it sinned against God. By choosing to live off the tree of knowledge of good and evil rather than the tree of life, Adam rejected God's plan for the human race. The tree of life represents the indwelling of the Holy Spirit, and when man rejected this guidance, it meant the human race could no longer know God intimately. Jesus came to repair this damage by dying on the cross and because he was God this act of his would have infinite value and could cancel any debt; and because he was man, he stood for the human family, bearing our sin and cancelling our debt.

What extraordinary truths are summed up in these very matter-of-fact statements. We express our belief that God so loved the world that he sent his only Son into it knowing that we would bruise him and cast him out of the city and watch him die. There is no word painting in these statements; they are a clear and direct declaration of our faith and we need to be sure that we do actually believe them.

Once Jesus had died the kingdom of death could not keep him captive for he was innocent, and so the Father called him to rise to new life through the power of the Holy Spirit. For the Christian everything centres round the fact that the Lord died and rose to new life, thus conquering death. Death is for the sinner, Jesus was innocent and so death could not keep hold of him. Because of his rising we have a certainty, that united to him, we, too, will die and rise to everlasting life.

We assert our belief that he is coming again to complete the kingdom that is already among us and to judge the living and the dead. We declare our faith and belief in the third Person, the Holy Spirit, who proceeds from the Father and the Son. The Father puts the whole of himself into the love he has for the Son; the Son puts the whole of himself into the love he has for the Father; the love between them is the Holy Spirit, a Person – God.

We accept that Jesus founded a universal Church through which the Spirit of God continues to make effective all that Jesus did by dying for the forgiveness of sins and rising that we might have eternal life.

Having stated our faith in the fundamental essentials of the Christian faith we now proceed to offer the sacrifice of praise to God.

5

Through Your Goodness We Have This Bread to Offer

The word 'sacrifice' denotes for most of us something painful, difficult, costly. We think of surrendering, giving up a precious possession. The word actually comes from two Latin words, 'sacrum facere', meaning 'to make holy'. The idea behind this was to take something you held precious and put it into the safekeeping of a god. This, clearly, meant being separated from your possession, but the object of the exercise was not so much the being separated from the possession as the putting it into the safe-keeping of a deity.

However, this basic idea of sacrifice became overshadowed by all sorts of other motives, and instead of asking for the safe protection of the object, the object became a gift to the deity for some favour in return. Thus the modern word now has the meaning of 'surrendering', 'giving up', and we do not think of 'making holy'. It is important for us to grasp the original and true meaning, and to realize that sacrificing something need not be a painful process. We can compare it to giving someone a present. Imagine giving the present and then bursting into tears because we have been separated from our gift. This would be to miss the whole object of giving the present – it was not to cause us pain but to give pleasure to the other, even if it means losing our gift.

At the Offertory in the Mass, we offer bread and wine. God does not need bread and wine, he is the Lord of the universe and he has no need of our gifts. What we are actually offering is ourselves, under the signs of bread and wine. These are good representatives because we all need food and drink to live. After hearing the Word of God in the readings for the day, we should all be ready to surrender ourselves, either in gratitude for his goodness or in repentance for our failures. In some way we want to put ourselves into God's safe-keeping.

We cannot all go up to the altar and give ourselves there and then to God, so we send up something to represent us. In some churches, as we enter there is a basket with hosts in it and beside it there is a silver bowl, and if we are going to go to Holy Communion, we place a host in the bowl. During the Offertory that bowl is brought up to the altar with the wine and water. While that is happening we should unite ourselves to the action by deliberately thinking of our gift of self to God. Also when the priest is offering the bread and wine, we should remember that we, too, are making that offering with him. Therefore if a hymn is to be sung at that moment, it should be a hymn which identifies with the action, so that we are not distracted from what we are doing. To sing a hymn to Mary or one of the saints would be to distract us from the action we are all involved in.

After the wine has been poured into the chalice and before it is offered, a drop of water is added to it. The prayer said at that moment indicates the meaning of this action. 'By the mystery of this water and wine may we come to share in the divinity of Christ, who humbled himself to share in our humanity' – the wine representing Christ's divinity and the water our humanity. Here we have summed up the mystery of God's plan for us. He calls us to be united with his Son. His Son became a member of the human race and was the first of that race to live, by his own power, without sin. When he died he became the sacrificial Lamb, taking the sins of the world upon himself and gaining forgiveness for them, and because he was God that action was able to cancel all sin. To stop us continuing in sin he offers to live in all those who accept what he has done.

There is absolutely nothing we can do to unite ourselves to Christ. We could not make ourselves worthy of such a thing. All we can do is to offer ourselves to God and invite him to come and unite us to his Son. The saving work of Christ has been completed – 'It is accomplished' – but it is not yet accomplished in us and in all those yet to be born. This is what Church is about, it is the family through which the saving work of Christ may be administered to the generations that succeed him. That is why it is so important to understand what is happening at the Mass. We are offering ourselves so that God will take us into his safe-keeping by uniting us to his Son and the offering he made of himself.

At one time people used to bring all sorts of gifts to the church, and at the Offertory these were brought up to the altar with the bread and wine. These gifts were to be distributed to the poor and needy. I saw this revived when I was studying French in Paris. At St Sevrin, a parish on the left bank, all sorts of goods were brought up at the Offertory. I then realized why the priest washes his hands after the offering of the bread and wine. At one time he would have collected raw vegetables and he would need cleaning up before going on with the Mass. The washing is now spiritualized, and as he washes his hands he asks for cleansing from sin.

Pagan and Old Testament Sacrifices

There are three main phases to a sacrifice: there is the offering of the gift or gifts; then comes the acceptance of the offering, the making it holy; and finally there is the communion with the gift that has been made holy. The actions surrounding a sacrifice are symbolic. In pagan sacrifices, and in the Old Testament, the gods or God did not come and take hold of what was offered, so some sign was shown to indicate that the gift had now passed into the possession of the deity. If the gift was an animal then its life was taken, and to ensure the carcass was not kept for food it was destroyed by fire. Here the gift was utterly taken out of the offerers' keeping. Sometimes it was the first fruits of the field that were offered, again these were often burnt as a sign of the gift being taken totally away. Primitive people thought that God or the gods needed these gifts, but soon the Chosen People began to see that the gifts they offered God stood for themselves. They were not allowed to take their own life, so they took something precious to themselves and let that gift represent themselves. By taking the life of the animal they were showing that they did not consider themselves worthy of their gift of life, and they offered the life of the animal in place of their own to make amends for sin.

In the Mass we, too, offer our life to God; we have sinned and we declare that death is our punishment and we want to put our life into the safekeeping of God. God takes our offering and makes it holy by changing it into the very offering that his Son made by giving his own life for the ransom of many. In the following chapter we will examine this extraordinary truth. But before we look into this mystery, we need to understand that at the Offertory we are asking God to accept our life and all its mistakes. The offering we make is not just bread and wine, we take these symbols and offer in reality our very self. And so the priest ends this part of the Mass by saying: 'Pray, brothers and sisters, that my sacrifice and yours may be acceptable to God, the almighty Father.'

6

Let Us Give Thanks to the Lord
Our God

 Having gathered together and asked pardon of God and one another; having listened to the Word of God and been brought again to that place where we want to surrender to him; and having offered ourselves to him under the signs of bread and wine – we now enter into the Eucharistic Prayer, the prayer by which we make present to ourselves God's great saving act of the death and resurrection of Jesus Christ.

This tremendous thanksgiving prayer begins with the prefaces. These are a variety of prayers used during different seasons and on different feast days. They are masterpieces, for they sum up profound truths in simple phrases. In some ways they sound too simple and we can easily slide over them and fail to see the fullness of their meaning. Because they are seasonal they emphasize the truth of the feast we celebrate.

During this chapter I will quote from the prefaces to indicate how they teach us the mysteries that

God has revealed to us. In these prayers the Church shows us what God has done for us and leads us to praise and worship him for his great power and love.

In the first week of Lent, we pray to the Father:

As we recall the great events that gave us new
    life in Christ,
you bring the image of your Son to perfection
    within us.

Here is a clear teaching on what holiness means and how we allow it to happen within us. It clearly is not something that we achieve, it is something that God achieves in us, and we open ourselves to it by calling to mind all that God has done for us in Christ Jesus. It is believing in the saving work of Christ that opens us to its healing power. Holiness is to have the image of the Son brought to perfection within us.

If we are to recall these great saving events we need to know what they are. God sent his only Son to bear the consequences of our sins. Death is the penalty for sin and so the Son of God came to die in our place. Before he could die for us he had to have a life that was capable of dying because as God he could not die. And so the Church teaches us in Christmas preface 3:

Your eternal Word has taken upon himself our
    human weakness,
giving our mortal nature immortal value.
So marvellous is this oneness between God and
    man

that in Christ man restores to man the gift of everlasting life.

And from Christmas preface 1:

In the wonder of the incarnation
your eternal Word has brought to the eyes of
  faith
a new and radiant vision of your glory.
In him we see our God made visible
and so are caught up in love of the God we
  cannot see.

When God sent his Son he did not send him as a new creation so that he could start the human family afresh, he sent him to be born from one of the daughters of Adam:

Through the power of the Holy Spirit,
she became the virgin mother of your only Son,
our Lord Jesus Christ,
who is for ever the light of the world.

Our Lady 1

God in his great mercy came to our rescue. We were incapable of making sufficient reparation for sin, so he sent his Son, who as God could make worthy reparation, and since he came among us as a man, he was able to be our legitimate representative.

We see your infinite power
in your loving plan of salvation.
You came to our rescue by your power as God,
but you wanted us to be saved by one like us.

Man refused your friendship,
but man himself was to restore it
through Jesus Christ our Lord.

Sundays 3

Christ sent his Son to be a second Adam, he came
to undo what the first had done. Adam lost life
through a tree, Christ comes to restore it by the tree
of the Cross.

You decreed that man should be saved through
the wood of the cross.
The tree of man's defeat became his tree of
victory;
where life was lost, there life has been restored
through Christ our Lord.

Triumph of the Cross

In these beautiful prayers we worship God by
reminding ourselves of his plans and also we are
instructed in what God has done for us, so that by
constantly being reminded of his love and care we
may enter deeper and deeper into, and thus open
ourselves to receive in an ever fuller way, the richness of salvation.

Liturgy is not theatre – it is not acting out scenes
from the past so that we may be spectators to them;
it is remembering, through words and signs,
moments when Jesus overcame evil, so that what
happened at those moments can affect us here and
now. This is made possible through the working of
the Holy Spirit, who has been sent to reveal to us
what Jesus has done, and when we accept what he

has done the Spirit brings the work of Jesus to fruition in us here today.

Eucharistic Prayers

There are four main Eucharistic Prayers together with several for children and reconciliation services. All these recall, in different ways, the death, resurrection and ascension of the Lord. Here, again, we find these prayers so packed with truths that we can miss their richness.

It was only after I had come to understand the centrality of the Lord's death and resurrection that I began to appreciate the Mass. It is so easy to think of the gospel as a code for moral behaviour. After all there are many injunctions to be good, truthful, loving. This turns the gospel into Good Advice, and not Good News – for it is discouraging to learn how difficult it is always to be loving and forgiving. The good news of the gospel is that through our union with Christ we can live in a new way. Union with Christ is not won as a reward for good effort, it is given to those who confess their weakness and throw themselves on the mercy of God who sent his Son to be our saviour.

In these prayers of thanksgiving we address the Father by calling to mind all that he has done for us through the work of his Son. Calvary is not repeated in the Mass, for that is impossible to do, but it is re-presented – made present to us, so that it may continually affect us. By listening to and praying these beautiful prayers, we are taught the fundamental truths of our faith. More important than the great miracles that Jesus did, more important than his teaching on morality, is the fact that God sent his Son to redeem us. He allowed himself to be besmirched with our sins and suffer the consequences, and thus paid for our sins more than adequately. But that was not all – death could not keep hold of this innocent One, and in obedience to the Father he rose up from the dead, thus conquering death. Here was the new Adam and from him the new human race would spring. So how fitting it is that we begin our thanksgiving to this loving Father with the words:

> Father, you are holy indeed,
> and all creation rightly gives you praise.

This is the very reason the Church has gathered us together. We have come to give thanks and praise to God for his mighty deeds.

Then we state what he has done:

> All life, all holiness comes from you . . .

This is a clear expression of the truth that we do not make ourselves holy, and the prayer goes on to explain how holiness comes to us:

> through your Son, Jesus Christ Our Lord . . .

Jesus is the One who took our human nature and made it holy and transmitted that holiness to us:

> by the working of the Holy Spirit.

Here, in very simple phrases, is stated the heart of

the gospel, and as we pray these prayers we should be saying to ourselves, 'That is true. That is true'.

Next, we present our offering to God, the offering we made of ourselves under the form of bread and wine, and we ask God to make our gifts holy through the power of his Holy Spirit.

And so, Father, we bring you these gifts.
We ask you to make them holy by the power of
    your Spirit . . .

At this moment we again offer ourselves willingly to the Father. All our cares, worries and weaknesses we surrender into his hands.

The only way that the Spirit makes anything holy is by uniting it to the Holy One, Jesus Christ, and we humbly ask God to do this for us:

We ask you to make them holy by the power of
    your Spirit,
that they may become the body + and blood
of your Son, our Lord Jesus Christ,
at whose command we celebrate this eucharist.

As a priest, now standing facing the people, I find this a very moving moment. We have all offered ourselves under the signs of bread and wine, and now as I say over the bread the words, 'This is my body', I see the people in the background and I am saying over them, 'This is my body' – the gift of ourselves that we have offered has been made holy by being united to the Holy One, Christ. In other words we have been Christed. The Holy Spirit of God is uniting us to Christ at the very moment

61

when he gave himself totally to the Father on Calvary. On Calvary, his body and blood were separated, causing death; on our altar, through the separate consecrations, his body and blood have been sacramentally separated, making Calvary sacramentally present, and we have been caught up into it very intimately. We now have the extraordinary privilege of offering to the Father the gift that his Son made of himself, with us caught up in that gift. The great prayer continues:

> Father, calling to mind the death your Son
> endured for our salvation . . .

What thought can we possibly find to call to mind that which has just been made real in front of us? Jesus heaving desperately on the Cross trying to catch his breath. Pushing against the nails in his feet to relieve the restriction in his chest, then sagging again once the pain of the nails in his feet became too great. God dying for his creatures. In a sense he is apologizing to his suffering creatures, by taking on himself rejection, suffering, abandonment, yet never opening his mouth to complain or draw attention to himself and what he is doing for us. A deep silence, not a word from him save that which had to be said.

We have but a moment to call this to mind, but that moment can be full if we have spent many moments pondering long on the mystery that God chose to die in our place. We cannot make this mystery touch us in the depths of our being. We may be able to stir our emotions, but that will not last. We can but stand, waiting till the Holy Spirit makes us know what our minds cannot know. Once this has happened a very quick calling to mind can be extremely profound and full. But unless we have pondered long, our calling to mind will be perfunctory, or alas, it may be no more than words while our minds are busy with their own affairs.

In the eucharist we celebrate the whole saving event, not just the death of the Lord, but also his rising and going back to the Father. So the prayer continues, calling to mind:

> his glorious resurrection and ascension into
>   heaven,
> and ready to greet him when he comes again,
> we offer you in thanksgiving this holy and living
>   sacrifice.

What an extraordinary privilege it is to be able to offer to the Father the gift his Son made of himself. Note the prayer says 'we' offer you. The whole people offer this living sacrifice to the Father. What an incredible honour! This is what is meant by the priesthood of the laity: all who are in the body of Christ are able to offer Christ's death and resurrection to the Father – a living sacrifice of praise. The ordained priest makes this sacrifice present on the altar, but the whole body offers it to the Father.

We now ask the Father to look favourably on this offering:

> Look with favour on your Church's offering,
> and see the Victim whose death has reconciled
>   us to yourself.

Here we state the central truth that salvation is not due to us for anything that we have done, but it has been won for us by the death and resurrection of the Son of God. He has reconciled us to the Father.

> Grant that we, who are nourished by his body and blood,
> may be filled with his Holy Spirit,
> and become one body, one spirit in Christ.

Because we are not holy of ourselves, we ask that we may be united more and more intimately with the Holy One through the work of the Holy Spirit. It is the Spirit's task to sanctify. He does this by revealing to us the truth, and as we accept it, he unites us to the Holy One, Jesus Christ.

We next ask that we be made a gift to the Father and thus join the family that the Son has won for him.

> May he make us an everlasting gift to You . . .

What an incredible thought that is – we become the gift that the Son gives to his Father; a gift bought at a terrible cost. And so we ask all the saints to interceed constantly for us that we may never fail to see the truth of the mysteries that we are involved in. The depth of these truths is infinite, hence we need to return time and time again to their reality and allow their power to penetrate deeper and deeper.

Having pondered with wonder all that God has

done for us, the human family, we now ask that it may have effect in the world of today.

Lord, may this sacrifice
which has made our peace with you,
advance the peace and salvation of all the world.

We remember the Catholic family, and we ask God's blessing on the Pope and the bishops and then we ask God to 'unite all your children wherever they may be'. I love the universality of this prayer, showing as it does the Church's concern for everybody. We also pray for the departed and we first mention 'our departed brothers and sisters' – and that means all Christians no matter to what Church they belong, for we are brothers and sisters in Christ. The prayer continues by asking God's mercy on 'all who have left this world in your friendship'. Again we see the catholicity of the Church; she cares for all who have died no matter what their belief may have been. If, in some way, they were in God's friendship, we have hope.

This great prayer of thanksgiving ends by stating the solemn truth that everything comes from the Father, through the working of the Son, by the power of the Spirit. The great 'Amen' should thunder back from the people, showing that they utterly and completely agree with all that has just been presented to them.

7

Give Us This Day

 Having called to mind and made present the great events that gave us new life in Christ, we now prepare to eat the eucharistic meal. We wish to identify ourselves with what we have celebrated. We have called the sacrifice of Christ to mind, now we call the Last Supper to mind, and by eating and drinking the sacred species, we unite ourselves to the saving act of the Lord.

Every year the Jews would call to mind the great saving event of the Old Testament. They did this by celebrating a meal, exactly similar to the one they ate on the night before they left Egypt. On that great night each household was instructed to take an umblemished lamb from the flock, slaughter it and mark the doorpost and lintels of the house where the meal was to be taken with some of the lamb's blood. Any house with this sign on its doorpost, would be passed over by the angel sent to bring death to the first born of each household.

Hence the feast celebrated every year after this was known as the Passover Feast.

The symbolism of the Feast is very marked, and the same symbolism is applied to Jesus. He was referred to by John the Baptist as 'the Lamb of God'. He was the Lamb without blemish who humbly allowed himself to be sacrificed for us all. A Christian is someone marked with the blood of the Lamb; we are singled out as people bought at a great price and therefore owned by God. The evil angels cannot actually touch us, unless we give them permission to do so. How fitting it is that Jesus introduced the eucharistic meal at the time when he and his apostles were celebrating the Passover. The great event by which the Jews celebrated their deliverance was used by Jesus to be the memorial meal by which we would call to mind our deliverance from the power of Satan. Jesus commanded us: 'Do this in memory of me.'

The Lord's Prayer

To help us prepare for the eucharistic meal, the Church puts on our lips the prayer that the Lord taught us. The very first word shows us that we are not here praying as individuals but as a People. It is God's plan for salvation that we be a people, a nation set apart, a body, united and vivified by the life of the Son. We are not united in the same way as members of a club are, we actually form one living body. That is why sins against each other are so harmful.

The reference to 'our daily bread' means both the bread we need every day and the bread of heaven given to us ordinary mortals for our spiritual lives, bread which we share in common. Saying Grace before meals is a help to remind us in our busy day how we depend on God and each other for our daily food. If there was no sun, no rain, no soil – how could we grow our food? If we had no farmers to till the land, sow the seed and harvest the crops – who would grow the food for us? If there were no markets, no traders, no sailors, no drivers – how would the food get to us? How easily we take so much for granted, which causes so much labour and work! Rightly we ask pardon for our offences, and we even dare to stipulate that we receive pardon in the same measure that we grant it to those who offend us. We end by begging God to protect us from all evil.

The priest continues after this beautiful prayer by asking that we be delivered from every evil. What a beautiful prayer of trust in the goodness of God that is. Evil can come to us in all sorts of forms and we simply ask God to deliver us from them all. This is a clear statement that we believe that God is the master of the whole universe. A clear belief that he is the One in charge.

The priest continues, 'Keep us free from sin' – again the prayer teaches us that it is God who saves us from sin. We certainly have to avoid putting ourselves in vulnerable positions, but it is God who saves us through the mighty work of Jesus Christ.

'Protect us from all anxiety.' What an evil, anxiety can be! We fret and worry and live as though God was absent, remote or powerless. Anxiety can eat away at the very heart of the gospel which tells us 'to fear not'. Anxiety can reduce us to a state of unbelief – and that is a serious place to be. The peace that Christ offers us is not the peace of this world, where all goes well, all is in harmony and we feel buoyed up with pleasure and satisfaction. The peace of Christ means to have utter trust in his Lordship. It is not a confidence that he is going to remove all our problems, though of course he is perfectly able to do so and may do so, it is a trust that he can make these problems life-giving. It is a peace that can exist in the midst of trial, a peace that rests on the promise: 'Be brave, I have overcome the world' (Jn 16:33).

The Peace

As we approach the eucharistic meal together the Church seems to wish to bring home the lesson that too often we are divided, so she makes us show the sign of unity and forgiveness. Vatican II wisely restored the kiss of peace to the whole congregation. At one time it was restricted to the clergy and servers, but now the whole people at Mass are encouraged to show this sign. It has been suggested that it is artificial to make this gesture to people we do not know, but then we do not hesitate to kneel next to people at communion whom we do not know, and receive the same Lord into our hearts. Because we are Christians, we all share in the same life, and the same food is at that moment nourishing us all. I know a very sad story involving an alcoholic, who, having stopped his drinking through the great work of AA, decided to return to Church. He had been away for many years and he felt a certain apprehension as he returned. Vatican II was still being introduced and when the time for the kiss of peace came, this person turned expectantly to the person next to him to extend the peace and was told 'I do not do that'. Sadly the remark was taken personally and the alcoholic was not seen in that church again.

The Breaking of Bread

For bread to be eaten, it needs to be broken; for wine to be drunk, it needs to be poured out. Ideally the bread used at Mass should be large and bread-like, needing to be broken so that it can be shared.

The bread we break has become the body of Christ, and as the priest breaks it we recall that Christ's body was broken so that we might be given life. After the priest has broken the bread, he places a small piece of it in the chalice saying, 'May this mingling of the body and blood of our Lord Jesus Christ bring eternal life to us who receive it'. This rite dates back to the fourth century, and we are reminded that as the sacramental separation of the body and blood portrayed the Lord's death, so the bringing together portrays the Lord's resurrection. Also this rite recalls an ancient custom whereby bishops expressed their unity in Christ with their priests and people by sending a small particle of the bread consecrated at their own Mass to be put into the chalice of the various communities.

We can recall in Scripture that it was often through the breaking of bread that the disciples recognized the Lord. There was, for example, the occasion when Jesus, unrecognized, joined the two disciples on the way to Emmaus, and although their hearts were burning within them they did not know it was Jesus until he broke the bread at supper. Another time was after Peter had spent a fruitless night fishing; the Lord appeared on the shore and told Peter to throw his nets to starboard. When all the disciples had hauled the catch ashore, 'they knew quite well it was the Lord. Then Jesus stepped forward, took the bread and gave it to them, and the same with the fish' (Jn 21:12,13). Here, the breaking of bread was part of the process by which the disciples recognized Jesus.

Another meaning to the words, 'Do this in memory of me', is that we, too, need to be broken and poured out for God and for others. How we fight against such a thought. We would rather work for the Lord, do great things for him, convert continents; but then whose glory are we seeking? The glory of God revealed in the face of Christ is the face of One broken, poured out, even wasted so that others might live. 'Come follow me.' Are we ready truly to follow Christ? So much spirituality can be seeking our own glory. This is the originating sin, the sin that refused to live the plan of God – 'be one as We are One' – and chose to live for the ego – to live independently.

The Meal Aspect

A meal is a very intimate gift, and, sadly, many of us have forgotten the deep meaning behind it. When we are given a pair of shoes, we receive something to use. It is the same with a book, we now have something to use. If we receive money, again we have something that we can use. But when we receive food, we are given the wherewithal to

live. The giver is, in fact, saying to us: 'I want you
to live.' This intimate sign is deepened when we go
to the trouble of preparing and cooking the food.
When we sit down and share the meal, we are
saying: 'I want to draw life from the same source as
you.' Jesus goes further than we can go, he becomes
the food and the drink. He is saying to us: 'Not
only do I want you to live, but I want you to live
through Me.'

Communion

Jesus instructed us to eat his body and drink his
blood, and so we boldly approach the altar, aware of
our unworthiness, but encouraged by his invitation.
Through the act of eating his body and drinking his
blood, we unite ourselves with all we have just
witnessed. We have offered ourselves to God under
the signs of bread and wine, these gifts were
accepted and transformed into the body and blood
of the Lord as he gave himself for us through death
when his body and blood were separated. We now
unite ourselves with this body and with this blood,
thus bringing them together again within us, signi-
fying his triumph over death – his resurrection. It
is in the power of this new resurrected life that we
live in a new way.

The priest at the time of preparation for communion says a silent prayer which beautifully sums
up all these truths. I feel it is a pity that it is said
silently – it may be that that was only a recommen-
dation for when the Mass was being sung, for the
Agnus Dei would be sung at that time.

The prayer says:

Lord Jesus Christ, Son of the living God,
by the will of the Father
and the work of the Holy Spirit,
your death brought life to the world.
By your holy body and blood
free me from all my sins and from every evil.
Keep me faithful to your teaching,
and never let me be parted from you.

How important it is that we are faithful to the Lord's
teaching and not other people's interpretation of it.

All who communicate express their belief and
desire to belong to Christ and the expression of him,
visible on earth, the Church. Jesus was insistent
that we come to the table of the Lord united with
each other:

> If you are bringing your offering to the altar and
> there remember that your brother has something
> against you, leave your offering there before the
> altar, go and be reconciled with your brother first,
> and then come back and present your offering.
>
> *Matt 5:23–24*

There are sins that arise out of the softness of our
human nature, sins of weakness – sudden anger,
sudden sexual desires, sudden impatience. Immedi-
ately following, we are sorry, repentant. But there
are also sins that arise out of the hardness of our
nature, these are sins of deliberate hate, unforgive-
ness, harbouring grudges, persistent unlove – these
are serious and, alas, can be hidden under a very
respectable and pious exterior. We should think
carefully before approaching the table of the Lord,

if we are in such a state and if there is not even a flicker of regret. 'Come to me, all you who labour and are overburdened, and I will give you rest' (Matt 11:28). In order to receive this rest, our coming to the Lord must be with regret and sorrow over our state.

The Church encourages a pause after the time of communion so that we may ponder and be amazed at what has happened. This is a time for personal adoration and worship, a time of quite union, a time for each to be with the Master. A time of incredible intimacy.

8

The Dismissal

The final part of the Mass is brief and that is significant. We came together to be present to Christ's everlasting sacrifice. We have been touched and enriched by it, now we are sent back into the market-place to carry out in our daily lives what we have just celebrated.

The time after communion is a quiet time, a time when we reflect on the intimate union we now have with the Lord. A staggering gift has been given to us, and those of us who receive this sacrament frequently can easily fail to grasp the enormity of the moment. I remember the first time I brought communion to a sick person, I was terribly conscious of what I carried, and then it dawned on me, how much more intimate it was to receive the Lord into my heart than carry him in my hands. How badly many of us need to rise from our complacency and consciously grasp hold of these realities.

The communion antiphon, which may be sung, read aloud or read privately, very often is like a word direct from the Lord. It is amazing how frequently the Scripture verse quoted is particularly suited for us that day. Sadly, however, we often fail to realize how privileged we are to receive such words from God; perhaps it would help us to imagine how honoured we would be if a distinguished person visited our town and sent a personal message to us! I remember once hearing the story of a lady who asked a famous preacher if he had a word from the Lord for her, and his response was to hand her the Bible. I certainly know from my own experience how easy it is to fail to see that every word spoken by God is a personal word for us.

During the Mass, we have listened and fed on the Word of God read to us in the Scriptures, we have also fed on the Word of God made flesh and made bread for us.

The priest ends the Mass with a prayer of thanksgiving and then he dismisses the people with the words: 'Go, the Mass is ended.' The word Mass actually comes from the Latin words of dismissal: 'Ite, missa est' – meaning, 'Go, it is the dismissal' (the sending out). I am afraid it is not exactly known how this word of dismissal came to refer to the whole celebration.

Before the dismissal, the priest blesses the people and although he says, 'The Mass is ended', in a sense he is saying the Mass is continuing. Christ came with the intention of healing us and setting us free, but he also commissioned us to go out and bring that healing and freedom to others. So, empowered with renewed vigour and life which we have drawn from this banquet, we go out now literally to do, in memory of him, what he did for us – to be broken and poured out for others.